RULES OF THE ROAD

WHAT YOU NEED TO KNOW ABOUT EMPLOYMENT LAWS IN MASSACHUSETTS

Emily E. Smith-Lee, Esq.

JONES MEDIA PUBLISHING

Published by: Jones Media Publishing
Printed in the United States of America by Author2Market.

ISBN: ISBN- 13: 978-1-945849-05-3

Contents

INTRODUCTION

I was on a conference call recently with some colleagues, a group of lawyers from other states and other practice areas who talk once a week about how our practices are going, share ideas, and sometimes commiserate. One says: "I just made a terrible mistake. I had to let go an employee who was a real problem, but I didn't warn her that if she didn't do [something] she would be fired. Now she is upset and I think I have opened myself up to a lawsuit."

Behind this simple statement lie some of the myths, truths, and half-truths about employment law that stymie many businesses and the people who work for them.

Myth: the law requires warnings, or "progressive discipline" before terminating an employee for a minor or moderate transgression.

Truth: in states like Massachusetts that are "employment at-will" states, if you do not have a contract that says otherwise, an employee can be fired for a good reason, a bad reason, or no reason at all, so long as the termination is not discriminatory or done in retaliation for the employee exercising a legally protected right.

Half-Truth: being in an "at-will" state protects an employer from lawsuits for firing an employee. My colleague in all likelihood did not violate any law in his handling of the termination, but was still correct that he may have opened himself up to a lawsuit. Why? Because (i) discrimination and retaliation are not difficult to claim, though they may be difficult to prove; and (ii) there are many other ways that a business can run afoul of employment laws, and a terminated employee who is angry about the process may well go looking for them.

The purpose of this book is to provide both businesses and their employees with a simple guide to their rights and obligations. I am writing for both audiences because from years of experience on both sides of employment disputes, I can say with conviction that there are employees who are truly wronged by their employer's actions, and also that there are business owners and managers who are trying to do the right thing by their employees but find themselves in trouble because they don't know the rules, or don't have an easy way to ask for help or advice before a situation gets out of control.

In the first two chapters, we cover issues that frequently come up around employment decisions like termination and discipline, and the rules everyone should be aware of concerning exceptions to the "at-will" employment doctrine. In Chapter Three, we cover wage and hour and overtime rules, a frequent source of expensive and distracting lawsuits. In Chapter Four, we address the often-misunderstood issue of when someone can be lawfully classified as an independent contractor rather than an employee. In Chapter 5, we cover the issue of non-compete agreements, another common source of disagreement between employers and former employees. In Chapter Six, we cover some issues and problems that we commonly see in start-ups and closely held corporations. In Chapter Seven, we cover the issue of unemployment benefits and what considerations might affect your decision about whether to contest a departing employee's eligibility. Finally, in Chapter Eight, we offer some practical advice to employers based upon our years of experience navigating employment relationships gone bad.

Chapter 1

TERMINATION AND DISCIPLINE

"At-Will" Employment

The voluntary, or "at-will" nature of the employment relationship is a key concept in Massachusetts employment law. Though the phrase "at-will" is often used as shorthand for an employer's broad discretion to fire an employee, the concept also has its roots in the laws against slavery and indentured servitude, and the idea that nobody can be compelled to work for anyone else. In its purest form, either the employer or the employee is free to say "this isn't working for me," even if it is only because they don't like the color of the other person's socks.

Massachusetts is an "at-will" employment state. This means that, subject to the exceptions below, an employee can be fired for a good reason, a bad reason, or no reason at all. This also means that, contrary to popular belief, there is no legal requirement that an employer use warnings or "progressive discipline" before terminating an employee.

Exception: Discrimination

If instead of terminating an employee because you don't like the color of their socks but instead because you don't like the color of their skin, most people understand that would violate the laws against racial discrimination, which arose to address a long history of unequal opportunity and treatment based on race. What many people do not understand, or at least do not have "front of mind" when dealing with a problem in an employment relationship, is that the list of protected classes is much broader than this, particularly under Massachusetts state law. These are:

- Race and/or Color (Federal and Massachusetts law)
- Religious Creed (Federal and Massachusetts law)
- National Origin and/or Ancestry (Federal and Massachusetts law)
- Sex (Federal and Massachusetts law)
- Age: over 40 (Federal and Massachusetts law)
- Disability or Perceived Disability (Federal and Massachusetts law)
- Pregnancy (Massachusetts law)
- Gender Identity (Massachusetts state law)
- Sexual Orientation (Massachusetts state law)
- Genetic Information (Massachusetts state law)

It is also important to note that there are other categories of people that might be considered a distinct "class" but are not "protected classes" under the law, including people with particular political views or affiliation, socioeconomic class, status as a parent, or appearance. An employer should still be careful, however, about treating employees differently for any reason other than job performance, as the law can evolve in these areas as well. For example, for many years obesity was not considered a protected class, but recently some courts have found it to be covered (in some circumstances) under disability discrimination. Similarly, though parental status is not a protected class, there are situations in which disparate treatment of a female employee who has small children might be fashioned into a gender discrimination claim.

This does not mean that an employee in a protected class cannot be fired or disciplined. It does mean that the employer needs to be prepared to demonstrate a legitimate reason for the action if it is ever challenged by the employee. Recall that there is no legal requirement for a system of warnings or progressive discipline, but regular use of these practices, including documentation of legitimate performance issues, can protect the employer from claims of discrimination where there was a non-discriminatory reason for the termination. Where evaluation systems, performance reviews, and disciplinary processes are consistently applied they can help protect an employer from legal claims, but if the systems are applied inconsistently, they might have little effect on the employer's exposure and in some cases can even do harm.

Two examples illustrate this point:

- An employee with a medical disability was fired. The company had a robust performance evaluation system, based on both objective criteria and subjective evaluation comments, which documented a prolonged period of dissatisfaction with the employee's performance. Though she was in a protected class (disability), the court found there was no evidence of discrimination, so the company had no liability.
- A female sales representative was fired for not meeting specific sales goals on a performance improvement plan. Though there was objective evidence that she fell short of expectations, she was the only female sales person in the group, and the

improvement plan itself set goals that were higher and more unachievable than the goals set for her male colleagues. The employer ultimately settled a claim of gender discrimination with her.

The lesson: a consistent evaluation and warning system can ensure fairness in the process and protect an employer from discrimination claims, but creating one to deal with a specific employee can backfire, and serve as evidence that the employee was actually singled out based on her membership in a protected class.

You should also be aware that acts short of termination can also implicate anti-discrimination laws, which apply to any adverse employment action. This means that demotions, differentials in pay, non-promotions and other similar decisions could give rise to a discrimination claim if an employee unhappy with the decision can prove a discriminatory motive. Also, in addition to the general laws against discrimination, there are federal and state statutes that specifically prohibit paying employees at different rates for equal or comparable work based on gender. An employee can make a claim under these laws without proving discriminatory intent of she can prove unequal pay for equal or comparable work and the employer cannot prove a legitimate reason for the difference.

Exception: Constructive Discharge and Hostile Work Environment

If an employer allows discriminatory harassment in the workplace that effectively makes it untenable for a targeted employee to remain on the job, that employee may resign and still bring the equivalent of a wrongful termination suit, under the theory known as "constructive discharge."

This concept is the source of widespread misunderstanding on the part of both employees and employers that workplace bullying and a "hostile work environment" are always unlawful. Not necessarily. This does not mean it is a good idea for an employer to allow this kind of behavior in the workplace, but it is only legally actionable in certain circumstances.

"Hostile work environment" is a term that only has legal significance in the context of discrimination and harassment based on a person's membership in a protected class (see above). A classic example of an actionable hostile work environment is one in which employees are permitted to display sexually explicit images in their workspaces, or persistently tell off-color jokes or stories in the presence of a female employee. The behavior, if directed specifically at the female employee, could constitute sexual harassment, and therefore the same behavior generalized in the workplace could be actionable as a hostile work environment.

In contrast, if a group of employees are generally hostile to another employee without any discriminatory intent, no matter how bad the behavior or how actually hostile the work environment is, it is probably not unlawful. The truth is most situations that an employee might label a "hostile work environment" fall somewhere in between these two extremes, and you may need legal advice to determine whether there is any legal claim that could arise from the behavior.

"Workplace bullying" is another term we hear a lot from employees calling to seek legal advice. It certainly happens, and is certainly intensely problematic for the individual who feels targeted by such behavior, but it is not- at least not in Massachusetts and at least not at the present- against the law. Some years back, Massachusetts passed a law against bullying in the schools to protect children, but no similar law has yet been enacted to protect adults in the workplace. While there are many, many good reasons for an employer to address and stop behavior that could be considered bullying, it is not an independent basis for a lawsuit. Be extra careful, however, if the target of the behavior is a member of a protected class (see discussion of hostile work environment above).

Exception: Retaliation

There are certain things employees have a legal right to do, things that are sometimes understandably inconvenient to the employer, but for which the employee cannot be punished. Examples include:

- Reporting a workplace safety concern to state or federal authorities;
- Reporting a workplace injury and/or applying for workers' compensation;
- Requesting or taking leave under the Family Medical Leave Act (see Chapter 2, Employee Illness and Disability);
- Making a complaint (within the company or to authorities) about sexual harassment and/or discrimination in the workplace;
- Making a complaint (within the company or to authorities) about not being paid their agreed wages, overtime, or commissions;
- In some instances, making a complaint about an employer's violation of the law (commonly called "whistle-blowing");
- Taking time off of work to serve on a jury; and
- Using earned sick time under the Massachusetts Earned Sick Time law (see Chapter 2, Employee Illness and Disability).

It is important to remember that an employee's report of discrimination or harassment is protected activity, even if the claim is found to lack merit, so long as the employee believed in good faith that he or she was being discriminated against or harassed.

This means, for example, if an employee makes a claim of sexual harassment, and the employer investigates and determines that the behavior did not constitute sexual harassment, the fact that the employee made the report cannot be held against her. This means not only that she cannot be terminated for making the report, but also that she cannot be punished in other ways, such as an undesirable transfer or change in working schedule.

Exception: Breach of the Implied Covenant of Good Faith and Fair Dealing

In every contract, including an employment contract (whether oral or written), the law implies an agreement to deal fairly and act in good faith. This exception sounds broader than it actually is. It does not override the concept of "at-will" employment, and it does not mean that simply acting unfairly or meanly makes a termination actionable. The primary situation in which it has been applied in the employment context is where an employee is fired just before becoming entitled to something of value- a bonus, earned commissions, a profit-sharing distribution or other scheduled benefit. It could also apply if an employee is fired just short of a vesting deadline, if the employee can establish that the reason for the termination was to deprive him or her of the claimed benefit.

Employer Obligations On Termination

No matter what the reason for termination, employers have certain obligations under Massachusetts law that are strictly enforced. These are:

- Immediate payment of all wages earned up to the time of termination. If an employee resigns, this can be paid within six days of the last day of work, but if they are fired, the employer should be ready with a paycheck that day.
- Immediate payment of accrued, unused vacation time. The law treats vacation time as earned wages that must be paid on termination. This does not apply to sick days or personal days, which can lead to confusion if the different kinds of time off are not carefully tracked.
- Information about applying for unemployment benefits must be provided to the employee even if the employer thinks they are not eligible. The employer can later make the decision about whether to contest an application for benefits, but the information must be provided to the employee.
- If the employee is part of an employer-sponsored group health plan, he or she must also be provided with notice of the right to continue participating in that plan for a period of time ("COBRA"). The employer is not required to continue contributing toward the premiums.

Chapter 2

EMPLOYEE ILLNESS AND DISABILITY

This can be one of the most difficult areas to navigate for both employees and employers. Illness and disability present obvious and often significant challenges to the individual employee, but can also create challenges for the employer, and the rules are not always straightforward. In this chapter, we provide a quick guide to four of the rules that are most important to understand: (i) the laws against discrimination based on disability; (ii) the related laws against discrimination based on perceived disability; (iii) the requirements of the federal Family Medical Leave Act ("FMLA"); and (iv) the requirements of the Massachusetts Earned Sick Time Law.

Disability Discrimination and Reasonable Accommodations

As we mentioned in Chapter One, disability is one of the "protected classes" under both state and federal anti-discrimination laws. It is a unique class, however, because unlike the others, some disabilities can actually make a person unable to do some jobs. A blind employee cannot drive a truck, for example, at least not currently, and a person with a severe back problem likely cannot perform a job that primarily involves heavy lifting.

The law therefore only requires employers to make "reasonable accommodations" for an employee with a disability. What is reasonable is very fact-specific, and depends on the nature and needs of the business as well as the nature and extent of the disability. Very common accommodations include the purchase of special chairs for desk workers with back problems, assistive technologies for employees with vision or hearing problems, or adjustments in work schedules. They can include transfers to other jobs within the company- for example, a blind employee can't drive a truck but may be able to perform other functions within his or her capability and experience. Whether the law requires that particular accommodation will depend, again, on whether it is reasonable under the circumstances. A court would not likely require an employer to create a new position that it does not need to accommodate a disabled employee, but if a suitable position existed and was unfilled, the employer might be required to consider transferring the employee to that role if he or she was otherwise qualified for it.

Remember too that what is reasonable will continue to change as technology changes. For example, today there are many more options to allow people with sight and hearing disabilities to perform the functions of their jobs than there were twenty years ago. Similarly, accommodations that may be unreasonable today may become reasonable, and therefore required, as technology evolves.

Perceived Disability Discrimination

What many people do not know is that the law also prohibits discrimination based on "perceived disability." This can be a confusing area of the law- what it means in its most simplistic terms is that if an employer takes action (discipline, termination, unfavorable re-assignment) based on a belief that the employee has a disability, they may be subject to a lawsuit. Usually this starts with some actual injury or condition, which the employer or manager assumes to be more limiting than it is. By way of an example, consider an employee who returns from leave fully cleared to work but the employer restricts their hours based on an assumption that they continue to be physically impaired, or terminates them based on an assumption that they cannot do their job. Such a step could be actionable as perceived disability discrimination. This is particularly tricky in the area of mental health, where the clearance to return to work by a clinician is not necessarily based on objective tests and measures, but by the provider's clinical judgment.

The Family and Medical Leave Act

Under federal law (FMLA), if an employer has 50 or more employees and the individual has worked at least 1250 hours over the past 12 months, the Family Medical Leave Act requires that the employer provide job-protected leave for 12 weeks for the employee's medical condition or that of his or her immediate family member, or for the birth or adoption of a child. It is also unlawful to retaliate against an employee for taking FMLA leave.

The important things to remember about the FMLA:

- It does not apply to every employer, or to every employee (see threshold requirements above).
- The leave does not have to be paid, though employers sometimes provide paid leave through short term disability insurance policies or otherwise as an additional benefit.
- The leave does not have to be taken all at once. An employee might take two weeks of leave at the beginning of the year

due to illness, another two weeks later in the year to care for a family member with an illness, and another 8 weeks for the birth of a child. So long as the employee does not use more than 12 weeks total, the FMLA continues to apply.

- The employer can require reasonable documentation of the illness in order to approve the leave.

Though an employer does not need to provide more than 12 weeks of job-protected leave, it cannot retaliate against an employee for using all 12 weeks. It is easier to get into trouble in this regard than you might think, particularly if an employee has performance problems after returning from leave. As described in the section on discrimination above, consistent attention to performance reviews and a warning system can be critically important in making sure any action in that situation is truly performance-based and cannot be considered retaliatory.

The Massachusetts Earned Sick Time Law

This is a relatively new development under Massachusetts law, which took effect July 1, 2015. Under the law, employers are required to provide earned sick time for their employees, including part time and temporary employees. Unlike many other employment laws, including the FMLA, this really means all employers- big or small- and all employees-part time, full time or temporary.

The basics are as follows:

- All employees earn an hour of sick time for each 30 hours worked, beginning on the first day of employment, up to 40 hours in a year.
- Employers with 11 or more employees (note that this means actual people, whether full time, part time, or temporary)

must pay the employees for earned sick time that they use, at their regular hourly rate. Smaller employers still must provide the time, but making it paid time is optional.

- The time begins to accrue immediately, but an employer can limit the use of that time until 90 days (calendar days) after the start of employment.
- It is not just sick time: time off under this law can be for the employee's own illness, but also for purposes of attending routine medical appointments or taking care of a child or immediate family member, or taking a child or immediate family member to routine medical appointments.
- Employers of any size may not penalize employees for taking earned time, for complaining that an employer's practices violate the earned sick time law, or for supporting another employee's exercise of his or her rights under the earned sick time law.
- Unlike earned vacation time, unused earned sick time does not have to be paid out to the employee at termination.

It is important to note that the earned sick time law is now part of the Massachusetts Wage Act. This means that it is enforceable by a private lawsuit in the same manner as non-payment of wages (see Chapter 3 below), and if a court finds that an employer has violated the sick time law, it is mandatory that the employer be ordered to pay three times the amount of actual damages, and required to pay the employee's reasonable legal fees and costs.

It is also important to pay careful attention to the anti-retaliation provision. This, too carries with it the possibility of triple damages and attorneys' fees, but it has implications that are even broader than that. Imagine you are a working parent who has to miss some number of days each year to take your child to routine medical appointments. Prior to this law, you could be fired for missing too many days of work- being a parent is not a protected class under the anti-discrimination laws, and routine medical appointments do not qualify as a "serious health condition" under the Family and Medical Leave Act ("FMLA"). Now, so long as you are using the time you have accrued under this law, you may be protected from being fired, demoted, or disciplined because you used that time. Or imagine you have a seriously ill child or spouse and need time to take care of them and help get them the care they need, but you work for a company with fewer than 50 employees, or you have worked for your employer for less than a year, meaning the FMLA does not apply to you, even for unpaid, job-protected leave. The earned sick time law gives employees some of that protection.

Chapter 3

WAGE AND HOUR LAWS

B oth Massachusetts and federal law have many rules about the payment of wages, which are strictly enforced. These include: (i) state and federal minimum wage laws; (ii) state and federal overtime laws; and (iii) Massachusetts laws requiring timely payment of wages. It is important to note that if an employer does not follow these rules, liability is strict (meaning the employer is liable even if the nonpayment was an innocent or clerical mistake that is not corrected), and the employer can be responsible for multiple damages and for paying the employee's legal fees. Many of these statutes also specifically allow an employee to bring an action on behalf of himself and on behalf of others (essentially a class action lawsuit).

Minimum Wage

In Massachusetts, the minimum wage is higher than the federal wage, and employers in Massachusetts are required to pay the higher amount. The Massachusetts hourly minimum for most workers was raised to $10.00 in 2016, and increased again to $11.00 on January 1, 2017.

Wait staff, service employees and service bartenders may be paid a service rate ($3.35 per hour in 2016 and $3.75 per hour starting in 2017) if they regularly receive tips of more than $20 a month, and if their average hourly tips, when added to the service rate, are equal to or exceed the basic minimum wage ($10.00 in 2016 and $11.00 in 2017).

There is also a separate minimum wage ($8.00 per hour) for agricultural work (defined as "work on a farm and the growing and harvesting of agricultural, floricultural and horticultural commodities").

Overtime Laws

Any employee who is not exempt from overtime laws (state and federal) must be paid at one and a half times their regular rate for any hours worked in a single week over 40. Penalties for getting this wrong can be significant: two or three times the amount actually owed to the employee, plus payment of the employee's legal fees and costs if he or she wins a claim for unpaid overtime.

First, some terminology: an "exempt" employee is one who does not have to be paid overtime, and a "non-exempt" employee is one who must be paid at one and a half times their hourly rate for weekly hours over 40.

What you need to remember is that in order to be exempt from overtime, (i) the employee must be paid on a salary basis and earn at least the threshold amount per week; **and** (ii) their actual duties (i.e., what they really do all day, not necessarily what their title is) fall within one of the "exemptions" under the overtime laws.

For many years, the threshold salary was $455 per week. This meant that as long as an employee was making at least that amount, they might be "exempt" if they were performing exempt duties, but anyone making less than that amount had to be paid overtime no matter what their job was.

The Department of Labor issued new rules that were supposed to take effect on December 1, 2016, increasing that amount to $913 per week- double the prior threshold (approximately $47,000 per year). The Department of Labor estimated that 4.2 million workers exempt prior to the change would, without some intervening action by their employers, become newly entitled to overtime protection.

Just a week before the new rules were scheduled to take effect, a federal judge in Texas issued an order prohibiting its enforcement nationwide. At the time of this writing, that order has been appealed by the Department of Labor, and is pending before the Fifth Circuit Court of Appeals. These recent events leave many employers scratching their heads- some had already adjusted their compensation policies in response to the new regulations, and for all, it remains unclear whether the regulations will ultimately take effect, and, if they do, whether their application will be retroactive to December 1, 2016.

The bottom line: if you have employees who earn less than $913 per week and are currently treated as exempt from overtime, you have some risk that they will at some point lose that exempt status.

In addition, remember that this amount must be earned on a "salary basis" in order for the employee to be considered exempt. It matters less what you call it than what it is- if the employee's pay is constant from week to week even though hours worked varies, that employee is probably paid on a "salary basis." If, however, pay is regularly docked for hours missed, it is most likely not "salary" even if it is called that in the payroll records.

Assuming the employee makes the minimum earnings and is paid a consistent amount no matter what the actual hours worked are, they are still only "exempt" from overtime if what they actually do all day is considered an "exempt" duty under the law.

This is where an employer can really start tearing their hair out. The exemptions are broadly stated in the federal overtime laws as "bona fide administrative, professional, or executive" duties. In addition to the piles and piles of court decisions interpreting what those words mean, the Department of Labor has a long list of specific duties that it considers "exempt" under this language. If you are fortunate enough to find the category that fits you in the statute or Department of Labor regulations (for example, there are specific rules for outside sales people, computer technicians, actuaries, and numerous other occupations), then you may have your answer.

Most people, however, are left trying to figure out how the "bona fide administrative, professional, or executive" language applies to their situation, which is often not a straightforward exercise. If in doubt, you will want to consult with a lawyer, because the test is very specific to the facts of each employee's duties. There are, however, some basic guidelines for what each of these exemptions means.

"Professional:"

- The employee's primary duty must be the performance of work requiring advanced knowledge, defined as work which is predominantly intellectual in character and which includes work requiring the consistent exercise of discretion and judgment;

- The advanced knowledge must be in a field of science or learning; and
- The advanced knowledge must be customarily acquired by a prolonged course of specialized intellectual instruction.

Examples of exempt professionals include lawyers, doctors, dentists, teachers, architects and clergy. There are certain categories where some are exempt and some are not, depending upon the employee's level of education. For example, engineers with an engineering degree would be considered exempt, while someone with the title engineer but not the degree would probably not; registered nurses and nurse practitioners would be exempt, but not LPNs.

"Executive:"

- The employee's primary duty must be managing the enterprise, or managing a customarily recognized department or subdivision of the enterprise;
- The employee must customarily and regularly direct the work of at least two or more other full-time employees or their equivalent; and
- The employee must have the authority to hire or fire other employees, or the employee's suggestions and recommendations as to the hiring, firing, advancement, promotion or any other change of status of other employees must be given particular weight.

Examples include "C-suite" executives as well as general managers. Be careful, however- just because the word "manager" appears in the title does not mean the employee is exempt if the supervisory parts of their job are secondary to other duties that are not exempt. For example, there have been successful class action suits against major retailers arguing that assistant store managers are not exempt because they spend more of their time doing what non-exempt employees do (i.e., stocking shelves, assisting customers, running the cash register) than they do managing other employees.

"Administrative:"

- The employee's primary duty must be the performance of office or non-manual work directly related to the management or general business operations of the employer or the employer's customers; and
- The employee's primary duty includes the exercise of discretion and independent judgment with respect to matters of significance.

The administrative exemption is one of the more difficult to apply, as it does not include the kinds of "bright line" tests found in the other two. In general, these are employees whose role is to support the operations of the business as opposed to producing or generating what the business sells. Examples include human resource staff, payroll or finance, accounting, marketing and public relations, and legal and regulatory compliance. Even within those areas, only those employees who have to exercise independent judgment on "matters of significance" will be considered exempt.

Here are some of the most common mistakes we have seen employers make in this area:

Mistake #1: Ignoring the salary threshold, especially now that may double what it was prior to December, 2016. If you remember only one thing, remember that anyone making less than the applicable threshold per week is not exempt. Even if they are the CEO.

Mistake #2: Putting too much faith in titles. If someone is called a manager but spends the majority of their time doing the same work as the people they supervise, they may not be considered exempt.

Mistake #3: Assuming that any workers who are paid on a salary basis are exempt from overtime. Salaried workers are only exempt from overtime if (i) they earn a certain amount of money each pay period regardless of hours worked; (ii) the amount they earn is above the threshold; and (iii) the work they actually do falls into one of the exempt categories (see discussion above).

Mistake #4: Not having a way of documenting hours worked. Even if employees are not paid on an hourly basis, it is still the employer's obligation to keep a record of their time. Not having these records can be very costly for a business whose non-exempt employees claim to have worked more than 40 hours a week.

Mistake #5: Using the wrong numbers. We have seen a number of employers who believe that if they pay their employees on a two-week payroll, they only have to pay overtime if the total worked in two weeks is more than 80 hours. This is untrue- overtime is calculated on a per-week basis, not based on the payroll period. For example, an employee who is paid every other week might work 25 hours the first week and 50 the next- although the total for the pay period is less than 80, that employee (if not exempt) should still be paid at an overtime rate for the extra 10 hours in the second week.

The Massachusetts Wage Act

What many people may not realize is that, in Massachusetts, if an employee files a lawsuit based on nonpayment of wages or salary and prevails, it is **mandatory** that the court award them three times the amount owed and order the employer to pay their legal fees. Please read that again-it is important. There is no "good faith" or "innocent mistake" defense to a Wage Act claim.

On top of that, the Wage Act states that: "No person shall by a special contract with an employee or by any other means exempt himself from the Wage Act." Translated: an employer has to follow the wage laws, even if the employee agrees to something else, even if it is in writing, and even if the employee is a sophisticated, management level person.

The most important rules, at a glance, are:

- Employees must be paid weekly or biweekly, within six days of the end of the pay period, meaning if a pay period ends on a Friday, the employee must be paid no later than the Thursday of the following week.
- Employees who are exempt from overtime laws (see above) may be paid monthly, if they so choose, but still must be paid timely.
- You may not deduct money from your employees' paychecks except as specifically authorized under the law. You may, of course, withhold taxes and pre-tax payments for benefit plans, but should be very careful about other kinds of deductions, such as deductions that cover expenses associated with the employees.
- If you fire an employee, you must immediately pay that person for all time earned as well as any accrued, unused vacation time. If the employee quits voluntarily, these amounts must be paid within six days of the last day of work.
- Officers and certain management personnel are considered "employers" under the Wage Act and can be sued personally by an employee claiming a violation.

These obligations are taken very seriously by the courts in Massachusetts, and numerous decisions have strictly applied these provisions even as they relate to highly compensated employees. Some examples to consider:

- A small startup company hired a manager as its third hire. Several months later, it became apparent that the company had only enough money to pay its rent, electric, and telephone bills for four to six months, but not enough to pay its three employees. The senior management, including this employee, discussed the possibility of closing the company but agreed that they would keep the company alive by deferring any salary payments until business improved and the corporation could afford to pay them. The manager later learned of the provisions of the Wage Act and asked for payment. Eventually, the company paid her, one day after she had filed a complaint. Because she had filed a complaint before being paid, even by just one day, the company was still responsible to pay triple damages and her attorneys' fees.
- An out of state staffing company had a Massachusetts office, and paid its employees pursuant to the laws and policies of its home state. Specifically, that company's policy was to pay employees seven days after the end of the prior pay period, and to withhold accrued, unused vacation time if the employee resigned without giving two weeks' notice. A Massachusetts employee resigned without the required notice, and was not paid vacation time. This unintentional mistake cost the company an amount equal to almost two months of that employee's salary, plus the company's own legal fees.
- A hair salon had a policy of deducting a small amount of money per customer from its stylists' paychecks to cover the cost of products used in the service. This is common practice in the salon industry, yet a court found that the deduction

could violate the Wage Act's prohibition on deductions not authorized by law, and that therefore the salon could be liable for three times the deducted amounts.

Commissions and Bonuses

Commissions are considered "wages" under the Wage Act, but bonuses are not. This can create some confusion, as different employers use different words for elements of their compensation plans. In general, if an incentive payment is based on an employee's own contribution to revenue (the most common example involves amounts paid based on sales made by the employee), it is a commission, regardless of what it is called within the company. If, however, the incentive payment is based on something else (performance evaluations, or a share of the company's overall profits or revenues), it is a bonus, not a commission, and not subject to the Wage Act.

What this means is that an employee can enforce a right to earned commissions under the Wage Act, which includes triple damages and attorneys' fees. An employer can set a commission policy that defines when a commission is earned- for example, upon payment by the customer, completion of service or delivery of product, or when a customer signs an agreement. If there is no policy defining the trigger, a court may default to the closing of a sale as the triggering event.

An employee may be able to enforce a right to certain kinds of bonuses under a contract theory (for example, if a bonus is not discretionary but something the employer has made a binding agreement to pay), but would not be able to invoke the additional liability provisions of the Wage Act (in other words, they could recover the amount of the promised bonus, but not triple damages or attorneys' fees).

Chapter 4

EMPLOYEE VS. INDEPENDENT CONTRACTOR

As you can perhaps tell from the previous chapter, it might be tempting for an employer to pay people as independent contractors rather than W-2 employees, in order to avoid the many potential pitfalls of wage and hour laws. This is a very risky proposition under Massachusetts law, which provides that any individual performing any services is considered to be an "employee" for purposes of Massachusetts labor and Wage and Hour laws unless the employer can prove all three of the following:.

- the individual is free from control and direction of the business he or she is providing services for;
- the service is performed outside the usual course of the business of the employer; **AND**
- the individual is customarily engaged in an independently established trade, occupation, profession or business of the same nature as that involved in the service performed.

It is important to understand that **all three** of these tests must be met. It is the second prong that has proven most troublesome for employers. Even if a person functions independently, and "freelances" for other companies in addition to providing services for the business, if what that person does is part of the ordinary operations of the business, the employer could be breaking the law by classifying that person as an independent contractor. For example, if I hire someone to paint my office, or plow the parking lot, those activities are not part of the usual course of my business as a law firm. If, however, I hire someone for 10 hours a week to do legal research, even on a temporary basis, that person is performing a core function of my business, and likely should be paid as a W-2 employee, no matter how few hours he or she works, or how temporary the assignment. Ancillary support services (IT consultants, payroll or accounting services) are generally permissible to engage on a contracted services basis, assuming the other tests are met (actual independence and provision of similar services to others), and assuming those are not your core business activities. Gray areas abound. If you operate a restaurant, it is likely that you can hire a webmaster as an independent contractor, but if you operate an online store, an argument could be made that the website is part of your usual course of business, and therefore should be managed and staffed by employees under the law.

It is truly surprising how many businesses in Massachusetts get this wrong, so you should not assume a practice of using independent contractors instead of employees is lawful, even if it is common in your industry.

The measure of damages in misclassification cases depends on the circumstances, but can include the value of benefits that W-2 employees receive, the amount of self-employment tax liability the employee has incurred by being classified as a contractor, the lost opportunity to collect unemployment benefits if terminated, and any overtime pay that person would have been entitled to as a W-2 employee. Further, because violation of this law is also a violation of the Wage Act, the employer could be liable for three times those damages, as well as the employee's legal fees and costs incurred enforcing the law.

Chapter 5

NON-COMPETE AGREEMENTS

Many employers require employees, particularly key technical or sales employees, to sign agreements not to compete with the employer for a certain period of time after their employment ends ("non-compete" agreements or "restrictive covenants").

In Massachusetts, courts will enforce non-compete agreements only if they are reasonable in time and geographic scope, supported by consideration, and only to the extent necessary to protect a legitimate business interest. There is a lot packed into that sentence.

First, what is a "legitimate business interest" that can be protected through a non-compete agreement? This is one place where the words used by lawyers do not have the same meaning you might give them in everyday language. For example, you might consider it perfectly legitimate to want to keep your competitors from employing someone you have invested a lot of time and money in training, but that is not enough, even though it has practical and very real consequences for your business. In the eyes of the law, to rise to the level of a "legitimate business interest," the harm you are trying to avoid must involve something more, such as the protection of trade secrets and confidential information or protection of the employer's good will with its customers and prospective customers. So, for example, a sales representative who has built up customer relationships over a period of years very well might be ordered not to compete for a period of time in order to protect your interest in the goodwill he or she has built up while working for your company. In contrast, a back office employee with no access to confidential information or customer-facing responsibilities, however capable and important an employee, likely would not be held to a non-compete agreement.

Second, non-compete agreements must also be supported by "consideration." This means the employee must receive something in exchange for agreeing to the non-compete. You can ask a new employee to sign a non-compete as a condition of being hired, but if you want an existing employee to sign one, you should be prepared to connect that to something of value beyond simply keeping their job: a raise, a promotion, or even a one-time bonus or stock offering should be sufficient.

Third, what is "reasonable"? It is important to remember that "reasonableness" depends upon the circumstances, and there is no bright line rule about how long a non-compete can last, or how far it can reach geographically, because both of those questions depend on whether the time or scope of the non-compete is reasonable in light of the interest the employer is seeking to protect. So, for example, a nationwide non-compete might be found reasonable if the affected employee had a nationwide sales territory, while a 25 mile non-compete might be found unreasonable for a hair stylist, whose range of influence while employed was much smaller than that.

Because there are no bright-line rules, and every non-compete is analyzed on its own facts, it is difficult to be certain whether any given non-compete will be enforced. By way of example, below are some reasons courts have found not to enforce these agreements.

No consideration: if an employee is required to sign a non-compete as a condition of being offered a job, the job offer itself is "consideration" for the agreement. Where, however, an employee is asked to sign an agreement after beginning employment, with no additional benefit offered, courts have sometimes found those agreements unenforceable for lack of consideration.

Material change in job duties or compensation: if an employee's duties or compensation change materially during his or her employment, those changes may invalidate the original non-compete, if a court determines that there is essentially a new employment relationship that requires a new non-compete.

Overbroad terms: it might be tempting for an employer to reach as broadly as possible in defining the post-employment restrictions, but that comes at a risk of a court finding that it is not necessary to protect a "legitimate business interest." For example, restricting an employee from working for a competitor for over two years, or nationwide when his or her duties were primarily local, would probably be found overbroad. Similarly, defining "competitor" more broadly than necessary to protect the employer's legitimate interest can place the agreement at risk. Note, however, that in Massachusetts and many other states, a court may simply re-write the terms of the non-compete to make it enforceable if it finds the agreement to broad, and then enforce the new, more reasonable terms.

Compensation problems: there is a basic principle of contract law that says a material breach by one party excuses performance by the other. In other words, the first party to breach a contract may not be able to expect performance by the second of other promises. Where this comes up in the context of non-competes is where an employer has not paid the employee all agreed wages or commissions. In cases like that, some courts have found that because the employer materially breached the terms of employment, the employee was excused from complying with the non-compete provision.

For each of these scenarios, there are court decisions enforcing non-competes and declining to enforce non-competes, but it pays to be aware of these possible reasons for non-enforcement. With respect to the compensation scenario, it is important to remember that many of those situations trigger the provisions if the Wage Act, including the provisions about triple damages and attorneys' fees.

Because of all of this uncertainty, it is worthwhile to consult with an employment attorney before signing a non-compete, either as the employee or the employer. It should not take an attorney with experience in this area more than a few hours to gather the facts about your business and employees and draft an appropriate non-compete or advise you about the scope and likely enforceability of the agreement you are asked to sign. In contrast, a legal battle over a questionable non-compete can cost many thousands of dollars, with uncertain results.

Chapter 6

Start-Ups and Closely Held Corporations: Special Issues

For the most part, the rules described above apply equally to all forms of employment. There are, however, some issues that deserve special attention for closely held companies and start-up companies.

Fiduciary Duty

It is not uncommon in small, closely held companies and start-ups for key employees to also have an ownership interest in the company. This can happen where key employees start the company together; it is also fairly common where a start-up has limited funds to compensate key employees at market rates, and offers equity interests as part of the compensation package.

What many of these businesses fail to appreciate is that the law imposes a fiduciary duty on fellow shareholders in closely held (i.e. not publicly traded) companies. A fiduciary duty means each shareholder owes to the others a duty of "utmost good faith and fair dealing." This is a higher duty than an employer generally owes to an employee. It does not replace the idea of "at-will" employment, but certainly can complicate it. If, for example, a majority shareholder wants to terminate an employee who also holds a minority interest, he or she will have to demonstrate a legitimate business reason for the termination, or else may face a claim that the minority shareholder was "frozen out" of the company in breach of the majority owner's fiduciary duty.

Deferred Compensation in Start-Ups

We have seen many well-intentioned start-up companies find themselves in trouble for the compensation agreements they have made with their original key employees. The start-up "team," knowing that some time may pass until either the company begins generating revenue or obtains outside funding, often agrees to defer portions of their compensation for a period of time. This is a logical approach under the circumstances, but recall the broad and often severe reach of the Wage Act- if the relationship sours and the employee sues the company, the deferred portions of his or her pay can become a huge liability for the company and its officers.

The good news is that there are ways to structure deferred and incentive compensation that do not violate the Wage Act, so long as everyone is paid at least minimum wage on a timely basis, using bonus and profit sharing instead of a deferred agreed salary. Remember that getting this wrong can be very costly- it is definitely worth consulting with an employment lawyer to make sure your compensation plan is legal.

Incentive Compensation

Recall that the Wage Act **does** apply to commissions, and **does not** apply to bonuses, and that whether something is considered a commission or a bonus depends on what it actually is, not what it is called. If you call your plan a "bonus," for example, but it is calculated according to sales an employee makes, it is in all likelihood actually a commission. On the other hand, if the incentive is based on the fortunes of the company more generally (a percentage of overall revue or profit, for example, or an amount payable when the company reaches certain financial milestones), it is more likely considered a bonus, and therefore not subject to the Wage Act.

There is an important balance to strike here: if you are seeking to attract top talent, you may do better with a compensation plan that is concrete and tied to a mathematical formula than you would with a lower salary and a discretionary bonus, as the prospective employee will discount the value of the bonus because it is uncertain. You can almost have it both ways, however, if you structure your bonus plan to be tied to the revenue or profitability of the business as a whole. Just remember that any commitment to a non-discretionary bonus could be subject to enforcement in a contract action, even if it is not subject to the Wage Act.

The importance of all of this is not because anyone intends to back down on compensation promises made to employees. It is important, especially in a start-up, because of all of the financial uncertainties in such a venture, and because of the potential liability of individual officers under the Wage Act. If despite best laid plans and best intentions the venture does not work out, and there are outstanding Wage Act liabilities, those can continue to haunt the individual entrepreneur long after the business venture closes.

Chapter 7

A FEW WORDS ABOUT UNEMPLOYMENT

The eligibility of a terminated employee for unemployment benefits is another area frequently misunderstood, or incompletely understood, by all parties. Here are some key points to remember:

An employee is not necessarily disqualified if he or she was fired for cause. Only those employees who are fired for (i) deliberate misconduct in willful disregard of an employer's interest; or (ii) due to the employee's knowing violation of a reasonable and uniformly enforced rule or policy of the employer are disqualified.

Like most things in the law, the standards are easier to recite than apply to a specific factual situation, for example, what constitutes a "reasonable and uniformly enforced" policy, or what is "willful disregard" of the employer's interest. You can be reasonably confident that an employee terminated for theft or workplace violence, or one terminated for continued absences or tardiness in violation of a written policy that has been enforced against other employees, will be disqualified. You can be similarly confident that an employee who is terminated for financial reasons, or simply for poor performance, will still be able to collect benefits. Closer questions arise when an employee is terminated for violating a company expectation that is not documented, or a company policy that is sporadically enforced.

Usually an employee who quits voluntarily is ineligible to collect unemployment, but there are exceptions here as well. First, if the employee can establish that he had good cause for leaving based on something the employer did (examples include non-payment of wages, in some circumstances a pay cut or a demotion or other change in job circumstances), he will be eligible for benefits. Second, if the employee can prove that she had "urgent, compelling or necessitous" reasons for leaving, she may still be able to collect. Again, these are very fact-specific inquiries, but examples could include workplace harassment that the employer failed to control, or health reasons.

For an employer, whether to contest a terminated employee's application for unemployment benefits is an important decision. On the one hand, every employee who collects impacts the rate the employer pays for unemployment insurance- like every other kind of insurance, higher utilization translates into higher risk and higher premiums. On the other hand, contesting unemployment benefits will usually result in a hearing, which involves additional cost and distraction to the employer. Also, a terminated employee who may or may not have some other claim against the employer can be more motivated to pursue those claims if his unemployment benefits are contested.

Chapter 8

JUST BECAUSE IT'S LEGAL DOESN'T MEAN IT WON'T GET YOU SUED

T his chapter is primarily for employers and business owners who may be reading this book. Over the years, we have fielded literally thousands of calls from people with stories about employment relationships gone wrong. Sometimes there has been an actual violation of the rules, and sometimes not, but virtually all of these callers have one thing in common: for one reason or another, they did not feel they were treated honestly or fairly by their employer.

These reasons include being taken by surprise by a termination decision (i.e., no regular performance reviews or warnings about performance issues), being spoken to harshly or rudely by a supervisor, believing that their employer did not fairly investigate whatever issue led to their termination, and feeling that they had been a victim of workplace bullying without any meaningful assistance or support from management.

As we have said previously, none of these things are illegal. But they do make people pick up the phone and call lawyers. And, as you can tell from this book, there are many, many ways that employers can make expensive mistakes unintentionally. It is the angry employee who will be looking for those mistakes, and you would be surprised how often they find them.

By way of example, we had a client who was terminated from her job after she had disclosed a potentially serious health condition. Her employer confiscated her cell phone and looked at all of her personal data. She had a colorable claim of disability discrimination, and we discovered a significant employer liability for overtime, but after the case settled it became clear that she never would have called us if she wasn't so upset about the lack of sympathy for her health scare and her phone. Dealing with those two issues differently in the first place would have cost her employer virtually nothing.

An employee who is motivated to find a basis for a lawsuit can cost your business significant amounts of money if they are successful. Moreover, even a baseless lawsuit is expensive, distracting, and simply not what most business owners want to spend their valuable time dealing with.

So: we have been talking about the law, but relationships matter at least as much as the legal principles we have tried to outline for you in this book. If you have to terminate an employee, if you are faced with a decision about how to handle an employee illness or disability, if you receive a complaint about bullying or harassment in the workplace, or if you are questioned about wage and hour issues, I would encourage you not only to re-read this book, but also to take a moment, and perhaps a deep breath, depending on the circumstances, to consider how you can deliver the news of your decision in a way that is most likely to be perceived as fair and compassionate. Even if you don't have to- I promise that will save you money and aggravation.

CONCLUSION

Thank you for taking the time to read this book. The employment relationship is one of the most critical financial and commercial relationships that either the business or the employee can have, and there are countless ways it can go wrong, even with everybody trying to do the right thing. I hope that we have provided information that helps you avoid some of the most common pitfalls.

As you can no doubt see from the information in this book, however, the exact application of the rules to your situation can be very dependent on the facts, and no guide is a substitute for individualized legal advice. If you have questions about any of these topics, or have an employment situation you need help with, please call our team at 781-784-2322. As our way of saying thank you for your investment of time reading this book, we will give you an hour with one of our employment lawyers at no charge to answer your questions and assess your situation- just mention that you have read this book to the staff who answer the phone and they will set up your consultation.

Sincerely,

Emily E. Smith-Lee, Esq.

ABOUT
Emily E.
Smith-Lee

Emily Smith-Lee has almost twenty years experience in civil litigation, including business, employment and consumer disputes. She was formerly a partner at a large Boston, Massachusetts law firm, where she handled business litigation, product liability and tort defense, contract and trade secret and non-compete claims.

In 2009, she started her own law firm, which became slnlaw LLC in 2016. Since starting her own business, Emily has represented individuals and businesses in civil litigation involving trade secrets, non compete agreements, business litigation, labor and employment law, and consumer protection law. She has helped employees invalidate or re-negotiate their non compete agreements, obtained settlements for dozens of employees in overtime, wage and hour, and employment discrimination lawsuits, and favorably resolved numerous business disputes. Emily also provides advice to business owners on employment and contract issues.

Awards and Recognition:

Massachusetts Superlawyers list, 2013-2016

Fellow, Litigation Counsel of America

Education

Attorney Smith-Lee graduated from Johns Hopkins University in 1993, and from Boston College Law School, summa cum laude, in 1996.